What do penguins eat? Why do they huddle together in groups? Who won the race to the South Pole? What happens on a research station in Antarctica?

Find out the answers to these questions and more in . . .

Magic Tree House® Research Guide

PENGUINS AND ANTARCTICA

A nonfiction companion to
Eve of the Emperor Penguin

It's Jack and Annie's very own guide to Antarctica.

Including:

- Emperor penguins
- Leopard seals
- Antarctic exploration
- Antarctica today

And much more!

Here's what people are saying about the Magic Tree House® Research Guides:

Your Research Guides are a great addition to the Magic Tree House series! I have used Rain Forests *and* Space *as "read-alouds" during science units. Thank you for these!!*—Cheryl M., teacher

My eight-year-old son thinks your books are great— and I agree. I wish my high school students had read the Research Guides when they were his age. —John F., parent and teacher

And from the Magic Tree House® Web site:

My son loves the Research Guides about knights, pirates, and mummies. He has even asked for a notebook, which he takes with him to the museum for his research.—A parent

The Research Guides have been very helpful to us, as our daughter has an abundance of questions. Please come out with more. They help us help her find the answers to her questions!—An appreciative mom and dad

I love your books. I have a great library at home filled with your books and Research Guides. The [Knights and Castles] *Research Guide really helped me do a report on castles and knights!*—A young reader

Magic Tree House® Research Guide

PENGUINS AND ANTARCTICA

A nonfiction companion to
Eve of the Emperor Penguin

by Mary Pope Osborne
and Natalie Pope Boyce

illustrated by Sal Murdocca

A STEPPING STONE BOOK™
Random House 🏠 New York

Visit us on the Web!
www.magictreehouse.com
www.randomhouse.com/kids

Educators and librarians, for a variety of teaching tools, visit us at
www.randomhouse.com/teachers

Library of Congress Cataloging-in-Publication Data
Osborne, Mary Pope.
Penguins and Antarctica : a nonfiction companion to Eve of the emperor
penguin / by Mary Pope Osborne and Natalie Pope Boyce ;
illustrated by Sal Murdocca. — 1st ed.
    p. cm. — (Magic tree house research guide)
"A Stepping stone book."
Includes bibliographical references and index.
ISBN 978-0-375-84664-9 (trade) — ISBN 978-0-375-94664-6 (lib. bdg.)
1. Emperor penguin—Antarctica—Juvenile literature. 2. Antarctica—Juvenile
literature. I. Boyce, Natalie Pope. II. Murdocca, Sal, ill. III. Osborne, Mary
Pope. Eve of the emperor penguin. IV. Title.
QL696.S473 O73 2008 598.47—dc22 2007041134

Printed in the United States of America
10 9 8 7 6 5 4 3
First Edition

For Virginia "Gigi" Berbrich,
with love

Scientific Consultant:

JAMES J. BREHENY, Vice President and Director, Bronx Zoo.

Education Consultant:

HEIDI JOHNSON, Earth Science and Paleontology, Lowell Junior High School, Bisbee, Arizona.

Very special thanks to Paul Coughlin for his photographs; and to the great team at Random House: Joanne Yates Russell, Gloria Cheng, Mallory Loehr, and especially to the superb team of Angela Roberts and Diane Landolf.

PENGUINS
AND ANTARCTICA

Contents

Dear Readers,

When we go to the zoo, we almost always head right for the penguins. We could watch them for hours. But we really didn't know too much about them. We had no idea that male penguins protected the eggs, or that penguins lived all the way from the equator to Antarctica. For our book, we decided just to focus on penguins that live in Antarctica. They endure weather colder than you can imagine. Their struggle to survive is amazing.

We couldn't wait to begin our research. Someday we might actually go to Antarctica, but to research this book, we headed right to the library. We found great books and

videos. Then we went home and started reading and taking notes. First we wrote down the names of all the penguins that live at the South Pole. Then we looked them up on our computer. There are thousands of great penguin sites! We also read about Antarctica. It is the coldest and harshest place on the planet! Finally we began to write. We had so much fun learning all about the magical frozen world of the penguin. It was a great trip . . . and we didn't even have to leave Frog Creek.

Jack
Annie

1

Penguins and Antarctica

Antarctica got its name from the ancient Greeks. At night, the Greeks studied the stars. They watched as a group of stars called the *Great Bear* rose high in the northern sky. The Greeks named the most northern part of the world *Arktos*, which is the Greek word for "bear." This later became our word *Arctic*.

They thought that since there was a North Pole, there must be a South Pole to balance it. They named the southern tip of the earth *Antarktos*, which means "opposite of the bear." *Antarktos* became *Antarctica*.

But it was not until thousands of years later that anyone set foot on Antarctica. The first visitors found an incredible frozen world, more amazing than anyone could ever believe.

The Land of Ice

Antarctica is about one and a half times bigger than the United States. The South Pole lies almost at its center.

Ice covers Antarctica's mountains and valleys. Ice covers almost all the ground. In some places, it is over three miles deep. Antarctica is surrounded by the Southern Ocean.

Antarctica and the seas and islands around it are called the Antarctic.

During the winter, when the seas

14

around Antarctica freeze, the extra ice makes the continent look twice its size. Seventy percent of the world's freshwater is in the form of ice that lies in and around Antarctica.

Coldest, Windiest, Driest

If you like cold weather, Antarctica is the place for you. It is the coldest place on earth. The temperature is usually 60 degrees or more below zero. The coldest temperature ever recorded was in Antarctica—almost 130 degrees below zero!

Air this cold will freeze a person's bare skin in seconds.

-130°F

OUTSIDE TEMPERATURE

Antarctica is also the windiest place on earth. Howling winds sweep down from its center to the coastline. Sometimes they blow 200 miles an hour. That's hurricane force!

The winds dry out the air so much that they turn Antarctica into an icy desert. It is even drier than the Sahara Desert. In fact, Antarctica is the driest place in the world.

There is an area called the Dry Valleys that has not had rain for over a million years!

Even though only two inches of snow fall each year, Antarctica has lots of blizzards. Blizzards are storms with strong winds and blowing snow. Antarctic winds blow the snow that is already on the ground. This can make it hard to see or even to stand up.

Snow never melts in Antarctica.

During the winter, Antarctica is always dark. In the summer, the sun never sets at all. The only creature that can live in this harsh place all year is a tiny insect called a *wingless midge*. Researchers who work there live in warm buildings that protect them from the weather.

History of Antarctica

Millions of years ago, Antarctica was very different. It was not a separate continent. It was part of a giant continent that scientists call *Gondwana*.

Gondwana included parts of what are now Africa, Antarctica, Australia, New Zealand, South America, and India. This landmass covered an area stretching from the *equator* almost down to the South Pole. Gondwana was rich in plants and animals. Dinosaurs and other animals fed on each other and on the many plants growing there.

About 200 million years ago, Gondwana

The equator is an imaginary line that runs around the center of the earth, halfway between the two poles.

began to split off into different continents and islands. Over millions of years, Antarctica slowly drifted farther south until it covered the South Pole.

All the trees and animals that lived on Gondwana eventually disappeared from Antarctica. By 30 million years ago, it had frozen into a vast sheet of ice.

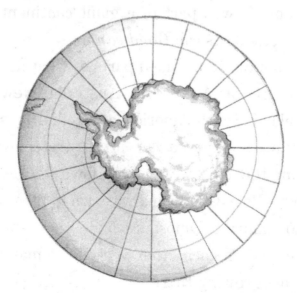

The Antarctic Circle is an imaginary circle around Antarctica and the Southern Ocean.

Icebergs

Sometimes tons of ice break off from high cliffs at the edge of the sea in Antarctica. This is called *calving*. It is an amazing sight. As the ice hits the water, ice crystals shoot into the air. They are like towers of white powder. When the huge chunk of ice settles into the sea, it looks like a floating mountain of ice.

These huge masses are called *icebergs*. One of the biggest icebergs today is over

183 miles long and 23 miles wide. That's the size of the state of New Jersey. And it's even bigger underwater!

Antarctica

Broke away from Gondwana
Once had dinosaurs and plants
Coldest, windiest, driest
Ice everywhere
Covers South Pole

The Busy Seas

Whales, seals, penguins, and other birds live in the seas and skies around Antarctica. In the summer, millions of penguins gather to raise their chicks. When winter comes, they head back to the *pack ice* and the open sea.

The continent of Antarctica is a lonely

Pack ice is floating sea ice.

place. Unlike in the Arctic, human beings have never lived there. The nearest land-mass is over 600 miles away in South America. The giant continent lies frozen and silent at the end of the earth.

Fossils in the Antarctic

Fossils are the remains of animals and plants that lived very long ago. There are many animal fossils lying under the ice in Antarctica. They come from the time when dinosaurs roamed Gondwana. There are also fossils of ferns and other plants.

Scientists make new fossil discoveries in Antarctica all the time. Recently, they were surprised to find the fossils of a duck-billed dinosaur on Vega Island, off the coast of Antarctica. They'd never seen fossils like these in the Antarctic before.

Another discovery at the South Pole was of a plant-eating dinosaur that lived 190 million years ago. This huge animal weighed over four tons and was twenty to twenty-five feet long! Scientists think it was the largest animal that has ever lived on land.

Can you believe there are also fossils of penguins that stood almost six feet tall? They lived over 6 million years ago.

2

Penguins

Many years ago, when explorers first went to Antarctica, they saw creatures they'd never seen before. They were not sure what kind of animals they were. These creatures spent most of their time in the ocean. They had wings but could not fly. Instead, they swam like the fastest fish and used their wings like flippers.

Some people thought the mystery animals were very strange fish. Guess what? They were penguins! And they are really birds. Like all birds, they lay eggs and have feathers and beaks or bills.

There are about seventeen different types, or *species* (SPEE-sheez), of penguins. They live in the southern seas all the way from Antarctica to the equator.

Penguins in the Antarctic spend most of their lives in the water. But once a year they live on Antarctica or on the surrounding sea ice to breed and raise their chicks.

Penguins live in huge groups called <u>rookeries</u>.

Over 100,000 penguins can gather together in one rookery. The rookeries are noisy, busy places. Penguins make noise to attract mates or to defend their territory. They spend time bowing to their mates, building pebble nests, waving their flippers, and grooming themselves.

Flying Through the Water

Penguins' bodies are made for speed in the water. Their webbed feet push the water aside as they swim. They use their stiff, pointed tails as rudders for steering. They really do look as if they are flying underwater!

Unlike most birds, penguins have heavy bones. This extra weight helps them stay underwater for a long time. The bones on their wings are flat and tightly fitted

 Some species can dive down 850 feet and stay under for 18 minutes.

together. They make great flippers! While they are swimming, the penguins leap in and out of the water. This gives them a chance to breathe. It also helps confuse any predator that might be chasing them.

When they leap out of the water, it is called porpoising.

Penguins are always on the lookout for food. They eat fish, squid, tiny shrimp-like creatures called krill, and other small sea creatures. Penguins don't have teeth. Instead, they have sharp little bristles on their tongues that keep the fish from escaping.

Fat and Feathers

Antarctic penguins need lots of protection from the cold. Extra layers of fat on their bodies trap in the heat.

Penguins have more feathers than most birds. Their short, thick feathers act like raincoats. There are little oil sacs near their tails. The penguins rub their beaks into the oil and spread it on their feathers. The oil makes their feathers waterproof.

When birds groom themselves or each other, it's called <u>preening</u>.

Penguins *molt* once a year. This means that they lose their feathers and grow new ones.

Antarctic penguins look as if they are wearing tuxedos. Their backs are black, and their fronts are white. To warm up, they turn their backs to the sun. Black draws in the heat and warms them up.

Penguins pant when they're hot . . . just like dogs!

When they need to cool down, they face the sun. White reflects the heat back into the air. Penguins also fluff up their neck feathers to release heat.

The penguins' black and white feathers protect them while they're swimming. When predators look down on them in the water, all they see is black. If predators look up at them, the penguins' white stomachs blend in with the water. Maybe their black and white feathers are even *better* than tuxedos!

Good Waddling

Imagine jumping more than two times your height!

Penguins leap from the water onto ice or rocks. Some can leap six feet high. If you see them moving about on land, you can't help laughing. They seem to have a hard time staying upright. Sometimes they hop. Sometimes they walk, often in long, straight lines. When they walk, they waddle from side to side. When they go downhill, they slide on their stomachs.

Research shows that penguins are actually very good walkers. They don't use up much energy. The emperor (EM-pur-ur) penguins of Antarctica sometimes walk over 150 icy miles from the sea to their rookeries. That's great waddling!

Predators

Early explorers killed penguins for their oil and for food. This doesn't happen anymore. But penguins still face danger from other predators. In warmer waters, sharks eat them. In Antarctica, both killer whales and leopard seals feast on penguins.

Leopard seals are the number one penguin predators. They can eat up to fifteen a day! When leopard seals attack, they often burst up through floating ice to grab an unlucky bird. The seals swim very quickly.

But penguins can swim even faster and sometimes escape. Leopard seals are the only seals that eat penguins.

Huge birds called <u>giant petrels</u> often eat penguin eggs and chicks.

Even though penguins are afraid of leopard seals, they are not afraid of people. If anyone gets near a rookery, the birds will rush up to get a good look. Since people have harmed penguins in the past, it's against the law to touch them. So don't even *think* about giving one a hug!

Some Antarctic Penguins
Adélie

Adélies are the most common penguins in Antarctica. They are small and weigh only eleven pounds. Like most penguins, the females lay two eggs every year.

Adélie

Chinstrap

Chinstraps are known by the thin black stripe under their chins. They make nests out of pebbles. They guard their nests very fiercely.

Chinstrap

Gentoo

Gentoo

Gentoo penguins have bright orange bills
and white marks on their heads. They also
have pebble nests that they guard carefully.
Sometimes they steal rocks from other
nests.

Macaroni

Macaroni penguins have a crest of yellow feathers on their heads. They get their name from fashionable Englishmen in the 1700s nicknamed "macaronis," who wore feathers in their hats.

Macaroni

Emperor

Emperor

Emperors are the tallest penguins . . . almost four feet tall. That's about as tall as a second grader! Unlike almost all other penguins, emperor penguins lay only one egg.

3

Daily Lives of the Emperors

Emperor penguins get their name because they look royal. They stand very tall and straight. Their yellow neck feathers and their black and white coat make them seem dressed up. Male and female emperors look alike.

In Antarctica, summers last from October through February. All other penguins breed and raise their chicks during those months.

But emperors breed at the end of April and in May. This is the beginning of winter in Antarctica. It is the harshest time of year.

Returning to the Rookery

Researchers have counted forty different emperor rookeries in Antarctica. Most are on solid sea ice. At some rookeries, over 100,000 penguins gather to mate. Other rookeries have only 200 birds.

When it is time to mate, penguins return to their old rookeries. They may have to walk one hundred miles or more to their old rookery. They face blizzards and *frigid* temperatures during their journey. The males arrive first. When the females finally arrive, the rookery really gets busy.

Courting emperors

Finding a Mate

The males try to find the same mates they had the winter before. That's hard to do with thousands of penguins milling around. The males make their own special sounds to find their old mates.

When the females approach, the males bring them pebbles to keep them interested. Then the males bob up and down.

If a male can't find his old partner, he finds a new one instead. In May or June, after about sixty-five days, the females lay just one egg. They pass it carefully over to the males.

Emperors don't build nests.

Now it's the males' job to care for the egg. The females make the long journey back to the sea. They will spend the winter feeding in the ocean. When the chicks are ready to hatch, the mothers return.

Meanwhile, the males remain behind with the eggs. They must wait eight long weeks until the chicks hatch.

Protecting the Egg

Each egg weighs one pound.

Males work hard to protect their egg. Just one mistake and the egg will break or freeze. The males quickly put the egg on top of their feet. Then they lean back a little

46

to cover the egg with a special flap of skin on their stomachs called a *brood patch*. If they can keep the egg covered, it will remain warm and safe. In fact, it will be as warm as a human: about 98.6 degrees.

A male emperor penguin protects the egg with his brood patch.

The dark and icy winter sets in as the emperors stand guard over their eggs.

Staying Warm

As the winds howl and the temperature drops, the males huddle in a circle for

Penguin huddles are called <u>turtles</u>. Can you guess why?

warmth. The group shifts around all the time. The males on the cold outer edge change places with the warmer ones in the center. When they walk, they must keep the egg between their feet and the brood patch or it will freeze.

Most of the time, the huge birds are quiet. The only noises you can hear are the roar of the wind and the cracking of the ice.

While the females are busy feeding in the ocean, the males don't eat. They live on energy stored in their body fat. During the winter, they lose about 40 percent of their weight. To save energy, they sleep a lot. Penguins can sleep while they are standing up.

At times, they sleep almost all day and night.

Sometimes the males are not success-ful in tending their eggs. Researchers often find eggs lying on the ground in penguin rookeries.

The Females Return

When the females return in August, it's time for the chicks to hatch. If a chick hatches before its mother arrives, the father feeds it with special food produced in its throat, or *gullet*. When the female arrives, the male carefully passes her the egg.

Then it is the males' turn to feed in the sea. Their journey back is difficult. They have not eaten for four months. The males are hungry and weak. Sometimes they have to travel several days to reach the sea. It is amazing that most of them make it to the ocean.

Six weeks later, they return to the

Adults travel back and forth from the rookery to the sea about six times.

rookery. Then it's time for both parents to take turns caring for the chicks.

Bringing Up the Chicks
When the chicks hatch, they are only six inches long. Instead of adult feathers, they have fluffy coats of gray feathers called *down.*

Newborn chick

The chicks arrive very hungry. They can't wait for their first meal! Their mothers have food stored in their stomachs. They bring it up and force it down the chicks' throats. For seven weeks, the babies need their parents' constant care. If they are left alone on the ice for just two minutes, they will freeze to death.

Joining Other Chicks

Crèche is French for a baby's crib.

At first, the chicks grow slowly. But at seven weeks, they can join other chicks in a big group called a *crèche* (KRESH). Just like their parents, the young penguins huddle together for warmth.

Now both parents return to the sea to feed. Each time they return, they call out for their young. The hungry chicks quickly waddle over to them. Often they'll try to get food from other adults. It doesn't work. Only their parents will feed them.

Danger

Young penguins face danger all the time. About half will die before they become adults. Many are victims of hunger.

Emperor penguins can live about 20 years.

Other threats come from seabirds like giant petrels and *skuas*. If chicks are weak or wander away, these birds are quick to grab them. When the chicks are old enough to spend time in the water, they also face danger from leopard seals and killer whales.

Return to the Sea

December and January mark the beginning of summer. The sea ice begins to break up. The penguins' walk back to the sea is much shorter. The chicks are growing up. Their downy coats are being replaced by adult feathers. It's time for them to leave the rookery and head for the ocean with their parents. When they get there, they are on their own.

These chicks are about to splash into the sea for the first time.

Penguins Near You

You don't have to go to Antarctica to see penguins. They live in zoos, aquariums, and wildlife parks all over the world.

But not many places have emperor penguins. They need a very special, cold environment. SeaWorld in San Diego has thirty-eight emperors. At SeaWorld, machines blow thousands of pounds of snow into the emperor exhibit every day! Visitors have to stand behind glass walls to avoid the cold.

Zookeepers have found that penguins can be playful. Some penguins try to untie their keepers' shoelaces. They also sneak up behind them and nip their knees.

Monterey Bay Aquarium

4

Animals of Antarctica

Whales, seals, and birds feed in the rich waters around Antarctica. Emperor penguins and Weddell seals remain in the Antarctic all year long. Other animals head to warmer waters in the winter.

Even in the summer, the Antarctic is cold. All the animals need extra protection to keep from freezing. They have thick layers of blubber, or fat, for warmth.

The larger an animal is, the more heat it

can store. Birds in Antarctica are usually larger than birds in warmer lands. Their size plus their waterproof feathers and extra fat help to keep them warm.

Some Antarctic sea creatures and insects have a special chemical in their blood that keeps them from freezing.

Seals live all over the world. About half live in the Antarctic. There are six species there. Seals come out of the water only when they mate and have their young. They spend most of their time in the water searching for krill, shrimp, and fish. During the winter, Weddell seals stay under the ice. In order to breathe, they cut air holes in the ice with their sharp teeth.

Some seals can dive down over 1,000 feet. They can stay underwater for up to thirty minutes! Before they dive, they inhale. Flaps on their noses close, trapping extra oxygen in their blood.

Seals belong to a family called <u>pinnipeds</u>. The word <u>pinniped</u> means "fin foot."

Whales are the biggest mammals in the world. Mammals are animals that feed their young on milk from their bodies.

Six species of whales live in the Antarctic. While they are there, they eat as much as possible. When winter comes, they leave for warmer waters to have their *calves*. They won't eat again until they return in the spring.

Baby whales are called <u>calves</u>.

Orca, or killer whale

In the spring, birds fill the skies over Antarctica. Millions of seabirds return to feed in the rich waters. During the summer, they mate and have chicks.

As winter closes in, they leave the Antarctic. Some fly all the way to the Arctic . . . the opposite end of the earth!

Now put on your warm clothes and meet some of the great animals of Antarctica!

Wandering Albatross

The wandering albatross has an eleven-foot wingspan. That's the largest of any bird. These great fliers spend almost all their life in the air. They can even fly at night when they are half-asleep!

Albatross often fly for months at a time without touching land. They rest on water instead. These birds cover thousands of miles by gliding on the winds. They do this by rarely flapping their wings. It's a great sight to see these gigantic birds swooping down in the ocean to catch fish and squid.

Albatross mate for life. They live long lives of thirty years or more.

Blue Whale

Blue whales are the biggest animals ever . . . bigger than any known dinosaur. They have the loudest voices as well. The noise of a blue whale makes a jet plane seem quiet! And you won't believe a blue whale's tongue—it weighs as much as an elephant!

When blue whales breathe out through their blowholes, they send showers of water fifty feet into the air.

Even though they are huge, these animals are often called gentle giants. They are not dangerous. Their main food is krill.

Blue whales live in small groups called *pods*. Some live to be over one hundred years old.

Leopard Seals

Leopard seals get their name from the blue spots on their coats. They are long and thin. The females are twelve feet long. The males reach ten feet.

Leopard seals have huge jaws. Unlike other seals, they have canine teeth that end in sharp points. Their jaws open wide and then snap shut very quickly.

Leopard seals are fierce hunters. They eat almost anything they can catch. This includes penguins, fish, krill, squid, and other seals. The seals hide in shallow water under an ice shelf. If they spot a penguin, they burst out and grab it. Their only enemies are killer whales.

Skuas

Skuas are relatives of seagulls. They are large birds with a wingspan of about four feet. They fly farther south than any other bird. Some have even been spotted at the South Pole.

Skuas are fierce hunters. They've been seen attacking other birds in the air and making them drop their prey. Skuas raid penguin rookeries for eggs and chicks. They also eat dead animals that have washed up on shore.

Skuas guard their nests by flying directly at the head of anything that tries to get too close. Researchers have to be careful to avoid getting hurt. The skuas' sharp beaks and open claws are dangerous. Nothing scares a skua!

Krill

Krill are the most important animals in Antarctica. They look like tiny pink shrimps only two inches long. Krill make up the diets of fish, whales, seals, birds, and squid. Without krill these animals would be in trouble!

Krill are part of the *zooplankton* (zoh-uh-PLANK-tun) family. They float in the water, pushed along by the ocean currents. Krill eat very tiny ocean plants. Sometimes they don't eat for over seven months!

Krill float about in huge numbers. Two million tons of krill can cover large areas of the sea. They look like a huge pink mass. If the weight of all the krill in the world was added up, it would be more than all the people on earth!

5

Famous Antarctic Explorers

For thousands of years, Antarctica was a land of mystery. No one was certain it even existed. There were no boats strong enough to get through the pack ice surrounding the huge continent.

But in the late 1700s, one famous explorer got close enough to guess that the Greeks had been right: land really does exist at the South Pole.

Captain James Cook (1728–1779)

James Cook was a great British explorer. He discovered places most people had never heard of. Captain Cook explored the Pacific Ocean, the Arctic, and the seas around Antarctica. He mapped the coastlines. He studied the movement of the earth and stars.

Long ago, sailors used the stars to help guide, or <u>navigate</u>, their ships.

Cook's Ships

Captain Cook's ships had flat bottoms that held a lot of cargo. The ships were so strong that he said, "No sea can hurt them."

Cook sailed around Antarctica on his ship the <u>Endeavour</u>.

The ships had crews of about one hundred men. Sometimes Cook and his crew battled raging storms, illness, and attacks from native tribes.

Captain Cook and Scurvy

Long ago, sailors suffered from a terrible disease called *scurvy* (SKUR-vee). It made their gums bleed and their teeth fall out. Many sailors became too weak to work. Some even died.

Captain Cook noticed that his men were healthy when they ate certain fruits and vegetables. He decided to make all the men eat lots of limes and pickled cabbage. None of them got scurvy.

These foods are full of vitamin C. The body stores vitamin C for about six weeks. After it runs out, there is a risk of getting scurvy.

Cook Gets Close

Captain Cook sailed around Antarctica, but he never saw land. There was too much ice for him to get close enough. Cook guessed that land was nearby when he spotted icebergs with rocks frozen in them.

But it was not until 1821 that a group of explorers from Britain actually set foot on Antarctica itself.

Robert Scott writes in his diary
inside his Antarctic hut.

Robert Scott (1868–1912)

In 1901, Robert Scott, another British explorer, landed on Ross Island, near Antarctica. He and his crew explored the area around the Ross Sea and spent the winter on the island. Although they hoped to see more of the continent, many of the men got sick. Scott sent them and some others back home.

In 2007, a rare colossal squid was found in the Ross Sea.

Robert Scott stayed behind to explore. When he returned to Britain, he was hailed as a hero.

In 1910, Scott went back to Antarctica. This time his goal was to reach the South Pole. No one had ever done this before.

 Scott was the first to fly over part of Antarctica in a hot-air balloon.

Scott set up a base camp and got to work preparing for his journey. But another explorer, Roald Amundsen, was making plans as well.

Roald Amundsen (1872–1928)

Roald Amundsen was born in Norway. As a boy, his dream was to explore both the North and South Poles. Young Roald slept with the windows open even in the coldest weather. He wanted to become hardy enough to endure extremely cold weather.

As an adult, Amundsen explored areas around the North Pole. In 1910, he vowed to reach the South Pole.

Amundsen knew that Scott also planned to go to the South Pole. Amundsen was determined to get there first. The deadly race was on!

Amundsen poses with his dogs.

A Race to the Death

Scott took off for the pole three weeks before Amundsen. He took ponies, some dog teams, and sleds run by gas motors.

Amundsen relied on dogs alone to pull his sleds. He had seen how well dogs endured the cold in the Arctic. He picked the strongest sled dogs he could find for his journey. Amundsen and his men set off.

Scott ran into trouble right away. Blizzards forced the men to stay in their tents. The ponies broke through the ice and died. The motorized sleds broke down, and food and fuel ran low. Scott sent the dogs and some of his men back to base camp. Scott and four others continued on. The exhausted men pulled the one remaining heavy sled themselves.

Scott and his men drag their sled toward the pole.

When they reached the South Pole, they were shocked. A Norwegian flag was blowing in the wind! Amundsen and his men had arrived three weeks earlier. The flag marked the Norwegians' great victory.

 Scott sees the Norwegian flag at the South Pole.

Frozen, hungry, and sick with scurvy, Scott and his men turned back. They died along the way. Eight months later, a rescue team came across their tents. The men lay frozen to death in their sleeping bags. They were only eleven miles from their next food supply.

Why Amundsen Won

Amundsen beat Scott for several reasons. First, he trusted his well-trained sled dogs. Scott and his men wasted all their energy pulling their own sleds.

Scott carried 35 pounds of rocks for research back with him.

Amundsen and his team got plenty of vitamin C. They took fresh seal meat, which was loaded with vitamin C. Scott's men lived on canned meat, which had none. When Scott and his team tried to return from the pole, they were starving and sick with scurvy. Amundsen's men actually gained weight on their trip back.

Amundsen and his men dressed in layers of fur. The furs were light and kept them warm and dry. Scott's crew wore mostly cotton and wool. Their clothes dried out slowly and were heavy when wet.

Amundsen's route was 60 miles shorter.

Amundsen took a shorter route to the pole than Scott. He made sure that enough supplies were stored along the way. Scott ran low on food, and the cans that held his fuel leaked.

Although he did survive Antarctica, Amundsen died in a plane crash years later. He was trying to rescue a friend and fellow explorer lost at sea. The friend was rescued, but Amundsen's body was never found.

Shackleton's Terrible Journey

Ernest Shackleton was in the Antarctic with Scott in 1901. He was sent home when he became ill. Afterward, Shackleton returned to Antarctica several more times. Once, he got ninety-seven miles from the South Pole before running out of supplies.

In 1914, Shackleton planned a 2,000-mile trip across Antarctica. He took along twenty-seven men. Among them was a photographer named Frank Hurley. Hurley took great pictures of the adventure.

Ernest Shackleton, far left, stands on the pack ice with his team.

Trapped!

When Shackleton reached the Weddell Sea, temperatures suddenly dropped. Ice froze hard around the ship. It could not move. The men were trapped.

Shackleton's ship, the <u>Endurance</u>, is trapped in ice.

The team lived on the ship for nine months. Then one day, it began to creak and groan. The ice was crushing the ship into splinters! As it broke up, the men escaped.

"She's going, boys. Time to get off!" Shackleton yelled.

The men lived in rowboats on floating ice for five months. Finally, the ice drifted into open water.

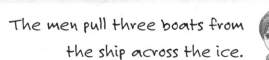

The men pull three boats from the ship across the ice.

The men set off in three small lifeboats. They rowed to Elephant Island, a frozen, deserted spot. Then they set up camp and planned their escape.

The men wave good-bye to Shackleton on Elephant Island.

Shackleton's Great Trek

Shackleton knew there was a whaling station on South Georgia Island. He and five others set out to find it in a tiny twenty-two-foot boat. They had to be careful to dodge floating ice. The exhausted men rowed against icy winds, pounding waves, and storms. They even went through a hurricane. Waves as high as fifty feet battered the little boat. The men guided their small boat by using a compass and a *sextant*. They could not use these instruments often because of the bad weather and the stormy seas.

Sailors use a sextant for navigating at night. It tells them where their boat is by measuring the distance between the stars and moon.

Finally, South Georgia Island came into sight. But their trip was not over. An icy mountain lay between the men and the whaling station. There were twenty-two terrible miles yet to go.

The men were rescued after four months on Elephant Island.

Shackleton and his men slipped and slid up and down the icy slopes. At last, they reached the station. A rescue ship left for Elephant Island. All of the men were rescued alive.

Shackleton's incredible ocean journey covered 800 miles. It took only seventeen days. What was really amazing was that they found South Georgia Island at all!

Antarctic Treaty

In the years to come, other people explored Antarctica. Many came to do research. By the 1950s, twelve countries had research stations there.

The treaty also says no dogs in Antarctica! They might spread diseases to other Antarctic animals.

In 1959, these countries signed the *Antarctic Treaty*. Later, other countries signed the treaty as well. They all agreed that no one country could own Antarctica.

It would be a place for peaceful research. The treaty says that no country can test military weapons there. No country can explore it for oil or other natural resources.

All the countries promised to cooperate and share research. Today there are many research stations throughout the Antarctic. Scientists from all over the world have joined together to learn more about this awesome land.

Turn the page to learn about an Antarctic volcano!

Mount Erebus

Imagine a volcano that throws lava bombs! Imagine a volcano that has beautiful ice caves and hundreds of ice towers! This volcano exists on Ross Island, in the Antarctic. It is named Mount Erebus.

The sides of Mount Erebus are covered with ice caves and towers. Heat and gases from the side of the volcano melt the snow and ice above and form ice caves below. Steam coming from holes in the earth's crust, called *fumaroles*, freezes into sixty-foot ice towers.

A large lava lake lies in the volcano's crater. Scientists think it might be miles deep. Mount Erebus erupts several times a day. When it does, it spews out lava that hits the icy ground and explodes. The lava lands like a bomb. Some of these bombs are almost ten feet wide.

Researchers say the temperature in the caves is always about 32 degrees. That's warm for Antarctica. Visitors just have to be careful to duck those lava bombs!

6

Antarctica Today

Most people who visit Antarctica go in the summer, when it is warmer. Some of the visitors are tourists. Others are scientists and researchers.

More than 20,000 tourists arrive by boat every summer. They travel with expert guides. There are no motels or hotels. They live on the ships. Whenever a ship stops, only one hundred people can go ashore. This rule protects both the environment and the animals.

Visitors to Antarctica see giant ice cliffs, mountains, and glaciers. They also watch

Goose-down pants and jacket

Really warm boots with crampons (spikes) to grip the ice

Camera with waterproof case

Waterproof gloves to keep out the water and cold

Extra-warm socks

thousands of birds and other wild creatures. They can even visit the huts that

Scott and Shackleton lived in. And while they are there, they breathe in the purest air on earth.

Shackleton's hut is still filled with his supplies.

About 1,000 people stay year-round in the research stations.

Researchers

When summer comes, about 5,000 scientists and researchers from all over the world arrive in Antarctica. Most stay only through the summer. They live in research stations or in camps.

Some of the stations are underground.

101

Antarctica is a great place for researchers. While they are there, they can study climate change, animals, the seas, outer space, and the continent itself. There is a lot of work to do.

For example, by looking at ice samples, scientists can tell how the climate has changed over millions of years. In the winter, the dark skies are perfect for observing outer space.

Daily Life on the Ice

Thirty-one countries have research stations on Antarctica. Planes carrying supplies have to land on snow instead of on concrete. They land on skis instead of tires.

The stations usually have several different buildings. There are labs for research. There are also buildings with bedrooms, libraries, dining rooms, and kitchens. People usually move from one building to another on snowmobiles or skis.

There are very strict rules for living at a station. No one is allowed to leave trash or anything else on the ground.

Life at a research station is not all work. Sometimes there are parties. The crews enjoy very good food. And the men and women spend time on hobbies like music, art, skiing, or reading. Some stations even have their own bands.

Everyone needs to eat a lot in cold weather to stay warm.

Camping on the Ice

Scientists sometimes work away from the stations. Small planes loaded with supplies drop them off far from their base. Sometimes they camp out as long as two or three months. The work can be dangerous. At times, thick clouds cover everything. The whole world looks white. It's like trying to see through milk. This is called a *whiteout*.

Crevasse

There are also *crevasses* (kruh-VASS-uz) to worry about. Crevasses are cracks in the ice—only, these cracks can go down over one hundred feet! And they can be hidden by snow. Falling into one of them is not fun! (You might not make it out.)

Scientists will never run out of things to learn about Antarctica. It is one of the few great wildernesses left on earth. It is a place of life and death. It is a place almost untouched by the rest of the world. A hundred million birds make it their home. Thousands of stars shine in the night sky. Huge whales call out to each other with earthshaking songs. Hurricane-like winds howl over the ice. And millions of penguins walk about with eggs between their feet.

Doing More Research

There's a lot more you can learn about penguins and Antarctica. The fun of research is seeing how many different sources you can explore.

Books

Most libraries and bookstores have lots of books about penguins and Antarctica.

Here are some things to remember when you're using books for research:

1. You don't have to read the whole book. Check the table of contents and the index to find the topics you're interested in.

2. Write down the name of the book.

When you take notes, make sure you write down the name of the book in your notebook so you can find it again.

3. Never copy exactly from a book.

When you learn something new from a book, put it in your own words.

4. Make sure the book is <u>nonfiction</u>.

Some books tell make-believe stories about penguins and Antarctica. Make-believe stories are called *fiction*. They're fun to read, but not good for research.

Research books have facts and tell true stories. They are called *nonfiction*. A librarian or teacher can help you make sure the books you use for research are nonfiction.

Here are some good nonfiction books about penguins and Antarctica:

- *Antarctica* by Helen Cowcher
- *Antarctica* by Allan Fowler
- *Hooray for Antarctica* by April Pulley Sayre
- *March of the Penguins* by Luc Jacquet
- *Penguins* by Seymour Simon
- *These Birds Can't Fly* by Allan Fowler

Zoos and Aquariums

Many zoos and aquariums have penguins. These places can help you learn more about Antarctica and the animals that live there.

When you go to a zoo or aquarium:

1. Be sure to take your notebook!
Write down anything that catches your interest. Draw pictures, too!

2. Ask questions.
There are almost always people at zoos and aquariums who can help you find what you're looking for.

3. Check the zoo or aquarium calendar.
Many zoos and aquariums have special events and activities just for kids!

Here are some zoos with penguin exhibits:

- Central Park Zoo, New York City, New York
- Lincoln Park Zoo, Chicago, Illinois
- Saint Louis Zoo, Saint Louis, Missouri
- San Diego Zoo, San Diego, California
- Woodland Park Zoo, Seattle, Washington

Videos and DVDs

There are some great nonfiction videos and DVDs about penguins and Antarctica. As with books, make sure the videos and DVDs you watch for research are nonfiction!

Check your library or video store for these and other nonfiction titles about penguins and Antarctica:

- *Antarctic Wildlife Adventures*
  from National Geographic

- *Emperors of the Ice*
  from National Geographic

- *March of the Penguins*
  from Warner Independent Pictures
  and National Geographic

- *Nature: Antarctica* from PBS

- *Nature: The World of Penguins* from PBS

The Internet

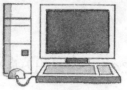

Many Web sites have lots of facts about penguins and Antarctica. Some also have games and activities that can help make learning about Antarctica even more fun.

Ask your teacher or your parents to help you find more Web sites like these:

- animals.nationalgeographic.com/animals/birds/emperor-penguin.html

- www.enchantedlearning.com/school/Antarctica

- kids.nationalgeographic.com/Animals/CreatureFeature/Emperor-penguin

- www.learninghaven.com/science/articles/penguins.htm

- www.livescience.com/penguins

- www.nationalgeographic.com/sealab/
  antarctica/place.html

- www.pbs.org/wnet/nature/antarctica

Good luck!

Index

Photos courtesy of:

If you liked
Monday with a Mad Genius,
you'll love finding out the facts
behind the fiction in

Magic Tree House® Research Guide

LEONARDO DA VINCI

A nonfiction companion to
Monday with a Mad Genius

It's Jack and Annie's very own guide to
the world of Leonardo da Vinci!

Look for it January 2009!

Guess what?
Jack and Annie are onstage!

For more information on
MAGIC TREE HOUSE: THE MUSICAL
(including how to order the CD!), visit
www.mthmusical.com.

Magic Tree House® Books

Other books by Mary Pope Osborne:

Picture books:

The Brave Little Seamstress

Happy Birthday, America

Kate and the Beanstalk

Mo and His Friends

Moonhorse

New York's Bravest

Pompeii: Lost and Found

Rocking Horse Christmas

Sleeping Bobby by Mary Pope Osborne and
    Will Osborne

First chapter books:

The Magic Tree House® series

For middle-grade readers:

Adaline Falling Star

After the Rain

American Tall Tales

The Deadly Power of Medusa by Mary Pope Osborne
    and Will Osborne

Favorite Greek Myths

Favorite Medieval Tales

Favorite Norse Myths

Jason and the Argonauts by Mary Pope Osborne
and Will Osborne
The Life of Jesus in Masterpieces of Art
Mary Pope Osborne's Tales from *The Odyssey* series
Mermaid Tales from Around the World
My Brother's Keeper
My Secret War
The Mysteries of Spider Kane
One World, Many Religions
Standing in the Light
A Time to Dance by Will Osborne and
Mary Pope Osborne

For young-adult readers:
Haunted Waters

MARY POPE OSBORNE and NATALIE POPE BOYCE are sisters who grew up on army posts all over the world. Today, Mary lives in Connecticut. Natalie makes her home nearby in the Berkshire Hills of Massachusetts. Mary is the author of over fifty books for children. She and Natalie are currently working together on *The Random House Book of Bible Stories* and on more Magic Tree House® Research Guides.

Here's what Natalie and Mary have to say about working on *Penguins and Antarctica:* "When we go to New York City, one of our favorite places is the Central Park Zoo. There are over sixty chinstrap and gentoo penguins at the zoo. These penguins are at home in the Antarctic, so their exhibit has to be kept cold . . . at freezing or below. The penguins spend most of their time in the water. But when they leap out onto land, you can really see how they act with one another. Some seem to spend a lot of time just hanging around.

"When we began our book on penguins, we didn't know how interesting and dangerous their lives were. It's amazing so many survive! So next time you see penguins, don't try to hug them . . . just yell, 'Good job! Keep those eggs warm!' "